Table of Contents

I. Introduction 3
   A. Brief Overview of the Significance of Money: 3
   The Central Debate: Is Money an Essential Lifeline or a Necessary evil? 6

II. Historical Perspective 9
   Evolution of Money Through Time: 9
   Commodity Money 11
   Metallic Money 13
   Paper Money 16
   Digital Transition 19
   Fiat Money 23
   Digital and Cryptocurrencies 28
   Historical Figures and Their Views on Money: 34

III. Money as an Essential Lifeline 37
   Role in Trade and Commerce: 37
   Providing Security and Stability: 39
   Facilitating Personal Freedom and Empowerment: 41
   Economic Growth and Development: 44

IV. Money as a Necessary Evil 47
   Moral and ethical concerns 47
   Income Inequality: 50

Societal Divide: Consequences of Income Inequality 52

Stress and Mental Health Implications 56

Corruption and Crime 60

V. The Solution: Balancing & Finding Middle Ground 66

Modern Ways: Money Management and Financial Literacy 66

Spiritual Ways: Money Management and Financial Literacy 68

I. Introduction

Money holds a unique place in our lives. It's a force that shapes our personal experiences, societal structures, and global interactions. At its core, the introduction will highlight the pervasive influence of money, setting the stage for a deeper exploration of its dual nature—whether it serves as an essential lifeline or a necessary evil.

In this book, we aim to grab the reader's attention by presenting the central debate. We'll briefly outline how money impacts our day-to-day lives, its historical significance, and its role in the broader economic framework. By doing so, we'll establish the importance of understanding money's true nature.

This book will serve as a roadmap, hinting at the nuanced arguments that will be explored in the subsequent book. It sets the tone for a balanced discussion, inviting readers to reflect on their perspectives and preparing them for a thoughtful analysis of one of the most critical aspects of human society. Also provide solutions via both Modern and Spiritual (Bhagavat Gita) ways

A. Brief Overview of the Significance of Money:

Money plays an undeniably crucial role in our world, acting as the lifeblood of economies and a cornerstone of personal and societal stability. It streamlines trade by serving as a common medium of exchange, eliminating the inefficiencies of barter systems. Beyond facilitating commerce, money offers a sense of security and stability, ensuring individuals can meet basic needs and plan for the future. It empowers people with the freedom to make choices, pursue interests, and achieve goals.

On a societal level, money is a driver of economic growth and innovation, enabling investments and job creation. Its significance, however, isn't without controversy. The moral and ethical dilemmas it presents, along with the disparities it can create, make it a complex, multifaceted entity.

By exploring the significance of money, we can better understand its dual role as both a vital tool and a potential source of discord, setting the stage for the broader debate on whether it is an essential lifeline or a necessary evil.

Money, in its essence, acts as the glue that holds our economic systems together. Its significance can be viewed through several lenses:

Medium of Exchange: Money eradicates the inefficiencies of bartering by providing a standardized medium of exchange. This convenience accelerates transactions and broadens the scope of trade, fostering economic interdependence on both local and global scales.

Store of Value: Money holds value over time, which allows individuals to save and plan for future needs and desires. This capability underpins financial systems and helps stabilize economies by enabling investment and capital growth.

Unit of Account: It provides a common measure of value, simplifying the process of pricing goods and services. This standardization is fundamental for managing complex economies, from setting salaries to creating budgets.

Economic Driver: On a macro level, money drives economic activity. It fuels innovation and entrepreneurship by enabling investments in new technologies and businesses. Governments rely on monetary systems to implement fiscal policies that stimulate economic growth and address economic downturns.

Security and Stability: Financial security is a cornerstone of modern life. Money enables individuals to meet basic needs, secure housing, afford healthcare, and provide education. It offers the stability necessary for personal and communal growth.

Empowerment and Freedom: With money, people have the autonomy to make choices that reflect their values and interests. This empowerment can enhance quality of life, fostering creativity and personal fulfillment.

Social and Cultural Significance: Beyond its economic roles, money often symbolizes status and success, influencing social dynamics and cultural norms. It can create opportunities for social mobility but also perpetuate inequality.

Moral and Ethical Dimensions: Money's significance also encompasses moral and ethical considerations. The pursuit of wealth can sometimes lead to ethical dilemmas, highlighting the need for a balance between financial ambitions and moral responsibilities.

Understanding money's multifaceted significance helps frame the central question: is it an essential lifeline that enriches our lives, or a necessary evil that complicates our existence? This duality is what makes the study of money so compelling.

The Central Debate: Is Money an Essential Lifeline or a Necessary evil?

An outline to the context and key details about the topic is money an essential lifeline or a necessary evil? is as below.

1. Essential Lifeline:

Facilitator of Trade: Money revolutionized trade by providing a common medium of exchange. Imagine if we had to barter everything—exchanging chickens for fabric, or corn for shoes. Money eliminates the complications of direct bartering, allowing for smoother transactions, better value assessments, and the development of more complex economies. This efficiency enhances productivity and makes global trade feasible.

Source of Security: Financial stability is synonymous with security. Having money ensures that people can meet their essential needs—food, shelter, healthcare, and education. It acts as a buffer against unexpected crises like medical emergencies or job losses. This security extends beyond individual households to entire communities, fostering social stability and reducing poverty.

Empowerment and Freedom: Money enables personal freedom and self-determination. It allows individuals to make choices that align with their values and desires—whether it's traveling, pursuing higher education, or starting a business. Financial independence provides the freedom to take risks, innovate, and grow, which are crucial for personal fulfillment and societal advancement.

Driver of Economic Growth: On a macro level, money is the engine of economic growth. It enables investments in infrastructure, technology, and education, driving development and innovation. Governments use monetary policies to regulate economies, stabilize currencies, and promote growth. Without money, funding for public services like healthcare, education, and transportation would be impossible.

2. Necessary Evil:

Inequality and Division: One of the starkest criticisms of money is its role in creating andperpetuating inequality. The uneven distribution of wealth leads to significant disparities in income and opportunity. This economic divide can create societal tensions and hinder social mobility, trapping individuals and communities in cycles of poverty.

Moral and Ethical Concerns: The relentless pursuit of money can lead to unethical behaviors, such as greed, corruption, and exploitation. This often compromises personal integrity and societal values. Corporate scandals, political corruption, and financial crimes are reminders of how the quest for wealth can overshadow moral considerations and lead to societal harm.

Stress and Mental Health Issues: Financial pressure is a significant source of stress and anxiety. The constant pursuit of wealth and the fear of financial insecurity can negatively impact mental health, leading to issues like depression and anxiety. This pressure can strain relationships, reduce overall quality of life, and even lead to burnout.

Corruption and Crime: The allure of money can fuel corruption and crime. From bribery and embezzlement to more severe organized crimes, the quest for financial gain often drives individuals to unethical and illegal activities. This corruption undermines trust in institutions and erodes the fabric of society.

II. Historical Perspective

Evolution of Money Through Time:

Money has undergone a fascinating evolution throughout history, transitioning from barter systems to complex financial instruments. Here's a brief journey through the ages:

Barter System

Before money, trade was conducted through bartering—exchanging goods and services directly. This system had its limitations, such as the need for a double coincidence of wants, where each party needed what the other offered.

The barter system is the most ancient method of trade, predating money by millennia. Here's a closer look:

Definition and Mechanics: Barter is a direct exchange of goods and services without a standardized medium of exchange like money. If a farmer had surplus grain and needed fabric, they would need to find someone with fabric who wanted grain. This mutual requirement is known as the "double coincidence of wants."

Historical Context: Bartering dates back to prehistoric times and was practiced by early civilizations such as Mesopotamia, Ancient Egypt, and the Indus Valley. It was crucial in communities where money had not yet been invented or was scarce.

- **Advantages:**
    - **Simplicity:** Barter is straightforward; goods are exchanged directly, eliminating the need for a currency.
    - **Value Based on Needs:** Goods and services are valued based on immediate needs rather than abstract monetary value.
- **Disadvantages:**
    - **Double Coincidence of Wants:** Finding someone with the exact goods or services you need who also needs what you offer can be challenging.
    - **Lack of Standard Value:** Without a common measure, determining fair exchanges is difficult.
    - **Indivisibility of Goods:** Some goods, like livestock or large tools, cannot be divided for smaller transactions.
    - **Storage and Durability Issues:** Some barter items, such as food, are perishable and difficult to store.

Transition to Commodity Money: These challenges led to the development of commodity money—items with intrinsic value such as livestock, grains, or metals, which were more durable and divisible.

The barter system laid the groundwork for more advanced economic systems by highlighting the need for a standardized medium of exchange, eventually leading to the creation of money. It underscores the evolution of trade practices from simple exchanges to complex financial systems we know today

Commodity Money

To overcome the inefficiencies of bartering, societies began using commodities with intrinsic value, such as gold, silver, and livestock. These items were durable, divisible, and widely accepted, making trade easier and more efficient.

Commodity money represents one of the earliest forms of currency, where items with intrinsic value were used to facilitate trade. These commodities had inherent worth, making them reliable and widely accepted as a medium of exchange. Here's a detailed look:

Definition and Characteristics: Commodity money consists of items that have value in themselves as well as value in their use as money. Common examples include gold, silver, grains, salt, livestock, and shells. For an item to serve effectively as commodity money, it typically possesses several key characteristics:

- Durability: It should last over time without deteriorating.
- Divisibility: It can be broken down into smaller units without losing value.
- Portability: It's easy to transport and carry.
- Uniformity: Each unit is the same as any other of the same type.
- Acceptability: It's widely recognized and accepted by people as a form of payment.
- Intrinsic Value: It has value even if it's not used as money, often because it fulfills a need or desire.

Historical Examples:

- **Gold and Silver:** Precious metals like gold and silver have been used throughout history due to their durability, divisibility, and intrinsic value. They were minted into coins, which made transactions easier and standardized.
- **Grains:** In agricultural societies, grains like barley were used as a form of money due to their necessity for survival and their storability.
- **Livestock:** In pastoral communities, animals such as cows or sheep served as currency because of their vital role in food production and labor.
- **Salt:** In some cultures, salt was so valuable for food preservation and seasoning that it became a form of money. The term "salary" even originates from the Latin word "salarium," which referred to payments made in salt.

Advantages:

- **Intrinsic Value:** Since these commodities are valuable in their own right, they maintain value even if they aren't used as currency.
- **Universal Acceptance:** Commonly needed items like metals or food were readily accepted and trusted, making transactions smoother.

Disadvantages:

- **Physical Limitations:** Commodities like livestock or grains could be bulky, difficult to transport, and subject to spoilage.

- **Inconsistent Value:** The value of commodities could fluctuate based on supply and demand or quality variations.
- **Non-standardization:** Without a standardized system, determining the exact value and making precise transactions could be challenging.

Transition to Metallic Money: Over time, the use of metals like gold and silver evolved into coined money. This transition marked a significant advancement, addressing some of the drawbacks of earlier forms of commodity money. Coins were easier to handle, durable, and could be standardized in terms of weight and value, facilitating more efficient trade.

Commodity money laid the groundwork for the complex monetary systems we have today. By using items of intrinsic value, early economies were able to conduct trade more efficiently and set the stage for the development of more sophisticated forms of money

Metallic Money

The next significant leap was the introduction of coins made from precious metals. Ancient civilizations like the Greeks, Romans, and Chinese minted coins that standardized value and simplified transactions.

Metallic money represents a significant advancement in the history of monetary systems, addressing many limitations of previous forms such as commodity money. Here's a detailed look:

Definition and Characteristics: Metallic money refers to coins made from metals that have intrinsic value, such as gold, silver, and copper. These metals were chosen because they are durable, divisible, portable, and have consistent value. The use of metallic money marked a critical evolution in simplifying and standardizing trade.

Historical Context: The use of metals as money dates back thousands of years. Ancient civilizations such as the Lydians, Greeks, Romans, and Chinese played pivotal roles in the development and widespread use of metallic coins.

Lydians: The first standardized metallic coins are attributed to the Lydians, an ancient civilization in modern-day Turkey, around 600 BCE. They minted coins from electrum, a natural alloy of gold and silver, stamping them with marks to denote authenticity and value.

Greeks and Romans: The Greeks further developed coinage, producing coins with intricate designs and denominations. The Romans expanded this system, creating a standardized and widely accepted currency that facilitated trade across their vast empire. Their coins, often made from silver and bronze, were stamped with the likenesses of emperors and symbols of state authority.

Chinese: In China, metallic money has a long history, with bronze coins used as early as the Zhou Dynasty (circa 1046–256 BCE). The round coins with square holes became iconic, allowing them to be strung together for convenience. Chinese coinage influenced trade and monetary systems across Asia.

Advantages:

- **Durability:** Metals like gold and silver do not corrode or deteriorate, making them ideal for long-term use.
- **Divisibility:** Coins can be minted in various sizes and denominations, allowing for precise and convenient transactions.
- **Portability:** Metallic coins are relatively easy to transport and store, especially compared to bulky commodity money like livestock.
- **Uniformity:** Standardized coins ensure consistent value, simplifying trade and reducing disputes over worth.
- **Intrinsic Value:** The inherent worth of precious metals like gold and silver adds trust and acceptance to the currency.

Disadvantages:

- **Resource Limitations:** The supply of precious metals is finite, and mining them can be environmentally damaging and labor-intensive.
- **Counterfeiting:** As coinage became more widespread, so did the risk of counterfeiting. Ensuring authenticity required sophisticated minting techniques and vigilance.

Economic Fluctuations: The value of metallic money can fluctuate based on the availability and demand for the underlying metals. economic systems:

- **Standardization:** Coins standardized transactions, making it easier to conduct business and trade over long distances.
- **Trust and Stability:** The inherent value of metals like gold and silver provided a stable and trustworthy currency, fostering economic confidence.
- **Government Control:** Governments and authorities could mint coins, thereby exerting control over the economy and standardizing currency use.

Transition to Paper Money: As economies grew and trade expanded, the limitations of metallic money, such as weight and supply constraints, led to the development of paper money. This innovation allowed for more flexible and efficient financial systems, paving the way for modern banking.

Metallic money's evolution from simple metal pieces to sophisticated coinage systems underscores humanity's ingenuity in solving economic challenges. It represents a critical step in the journey toward the complex financial systems we have today.

Paper Money

Originating in China during the Tang Dynasty (618–907 AD) and popularized during the Song Dynasty (960–1279 AD), paper money represented a promissory note or receipt for commodities held in reserve. This innovation spread to the Middle East and Europe, revolutionizing trade and finance.

Paper money marks a pivotal transition in the history of monetary systems, introducing a more flexible and efficient means of conducting transactions. Let's delve into its evolution and impact:

Origins and Early Use:

China's Innovation: Paper money was first developed in China during the Tang Dynasty (618–907 AD) and gained prominence during the Song Dynasty (960–1279 AD). The Chinese government issued these notes, known as *jiaozi*, as a solution to the growing need for a convenient and portable currency. Initially, they represented a promise to pay a certain amount of precious metals or commodities.

Mongol Empire Expansion: The use of paper money spread to the Middle East and Europe via the Mongol Empire in the 13th century. The famous traveler Marco Polo documented the use of paper currency in the Yuan Dynasty, marveling at its practicality and widespread acceptance.

Characteristics of Early Paper Money:

Promissory Notes: Early paper money functioned as promissory notes, where the issuer promised to pay the bearer a specific amount of gold, silver, or other valuables.

Government Issuance: Governments or state-backed banks typically issued paper money to maintain control and trust in the currency.

Portability and Convenience: Compared to metallic money, paper notes were lightweight and easier to transport in large amounts, facilitating trade and commerce.

Advantages of Paper Money:

- **Ease of Transport:** Paper money is lightweight and portable, making it convenient for carrying and large transactions.
- **Facilitates Large-Scale Trade:** Its convenience and ease of use enabled more complex and extensive commercial activities, boosting economic growth.
- **Government Control:** Issuance by centralized authorities allowed better regulation and control over the money supply, helping to manage inflation and stabilize economies.
- **Reduction in Coin Minting Costs:** Producing paper money was generally cheaper than minting coins from precious metals, freeing up resources for other uses.

Challenges and Disadvantages:

- **Counterfeiting:** The main challenge was the risk of counterfeiting, which could undermine trust in the currency. This led to the development of intricate designs, watermarks, and other security features to deter forgery.
- **Inflation Risk:** Overprinting or excessive issuance of paper money could lead to inflation, diminishing the currency's value. This required careful management by the issuing authorities.
- **Banknotes:** Over time, paper money evolved into standardized banknotes, which were widely adopted across the world. Central banks issued these notes, and they were backed by the promise of being

convertible into precious metals, such as the gold standard.
- **Fiat Money:** In the 20th century, many countries transitioned to fiat money, where the value of the currency is not backed by physical commodities but by the government's declaration that it holds value. This system allows for more flexible monetary policy but requires strong governance to maintain stability.

Digital Transition

The advent of digital banking and electronic payment systems has further transformed how paper money is used. While physical banknotes are still in circulation, a significant portion of transactions now occurs digitally.

Trust and Acceptance: Initially, building trust in paper money required significant effort, as people were accustomed to commodities with intrinsic value.

Evolution and Modern Use: Paper money represented a transformative leap in the history of currency, offering flexibility, convenience, and the ability to support more complex economic activities. Its development paved the way for the sophisticated financial systems we have today, where digital and electronic forms of money are becoming increasingly prevalent.

Think about our current digital wallets. Could you imagine living in the Tang Dynasty and witnessing the birth of paper money? Such a leap in human innovation!

Banknotes and Banking Systems

As trade expanded, so did the need for more sophisticated financial systems. Banks emerged, issuing banknotes that could be exchanged for precious metals. This practice laid the groundwork for modern banking and central banks.

1. Origins and Development of Banknotes:

Early Promissory Notes: The concept of paper money evolved from promissory notes issued by merchants and goldsmiths in medieval Europe. These notes represented a promise to pay the bearer a certain amount of gold or silver on demand, making transactions safer and more convenient by reducing the need to carry heavy coins.

Chinese Innovation: As previously mentioned, China was the first to develop paper money. The Chinese government issued these notes during the Tang and Song dynasties, which facilitated trade and economic expansion.

European Adoption: In Europe, the use of promissory notes expanded during the Renaissance. These notes evolved into banknotes when banks began issuing them as a form of currency. The first recorded instance of banknotes in Europe was by Stockholms Banco in Sweden, founded in 1656.

Central Banks and Standardization:

Bank of England: Established in 1694, the Bank of England played a pivotal role in the development and standardization of banknotes. It began issuing standardized notes that became widely accepted and trusted.

Other Central Banks: Following the example of the Bank of England, other countries established central banks that issued banknotes, creating a more stable and reliable currency system.

2. The Evolution of Banking Systems:

Medieval and Renaissance Banking: Early banks in medieval and Renaissance Europe were established by merchants and wealthy families, such as the Medici family in Italy. These banks facilitated trade by providing loans, accepting deposits, and issuing promissory notes.

Modern Banking Systems:

Central Banks: Central banks, like the Federal Reserve in the United States or the European Central Bank, play a crucial role in modern economies. They issue currency, regulate the money supply, and implement monetary policy to maintain economic stability.

Commercial Banks: Commercial banks provide a range of services to individuals and businesses, including accepting deposits, providing loans, and offering investment products. They operate under the regulatory framework established by central banks.

Investment Banks: Investment banks specialize in large and complex financial transactions, such as underwriting new debt and equity securities, facilitating mergers and acquisitions, and providing financial advisory services.

3. Functions of Modern Banking Systems:

Deposit and Lending Services: Banks accept deposits from individuals and businesses, offering a safe place to store money. They use these deposits to provide loans, which fuel economic growth by enabling businesses to invest and expand.

Payment and Transaction Services: Banks facilitate payments and transactions through checks, electronic transfers, and credit/debit cards. These services are essential for the smooth functioning of modern economies.

Investment Services: Banks offer various investment products, including savings accounts, certificates of deposit (CDs), and mutual funds, helping individuals grow their wealth.

Monetary Policy Implementation: Central banks regulate the money supply and interest rates to maintain economic stability. They use tools like open market operations, reserve requirements, and discount rates to influence economic activity.

Financial Stability and Regulation: Central banks and regulatory authorities oversee the banking system to ensure its stability and integrity. They implement regulations to prevent fraud, protect consumers, and maintain confidence in the financial system.

4. Impact on Economy and Society:

Economic Growth: Banking systems provide the financial infrastructure necessary for economic growth. They facilitate investment, entrepreneurship, and innovation, driving economic development.

Wealth Distribution: Banks play a role in the distribution of wealth by providing access to credit and investment opportunities. However, disparities in access to financial services can contribute to economic inequality.

Globalization: Modern banking systems have enabled the globalization of trade and finance. Banks facilitate international transactions, foreign investments, and the flow of capital across borders.

Technological Advancements: The banking industry has embraced technology, leading to the development of digital banking, online transactions, and fintech innovations. These advancements have increased convenience and accessibility for consumers.

The evolution of banknotes and banking systems represents a significant milestone in the history of money. From early promissory notes to modern central banks, these innovations have transformed the way we conduct transactions and manage economies. The banking system's role in facilitating trade, promoting economic growth, and ensuring financial stability underscores its importance in our daily lives and the global economy

Fiat Money

In the 20th century, most countries moved away from the gold standard to fiat money—currency that has value because governments declare it legal tender. This shift allowed for greater flexibility in monetary policy but also introduced new challenges like inflation control.

Fiat money represents a significant shift from commodity-based currencies to a system where the value of money is not derived from physical commodities like gold or silver, but rather from government decree. Here's a detailed exploration:

Definition and Characteristics:

- **Fiat Money:** Fiat money is a type of currency that has no intrinsic value and is not backed by a physical commodity. Instead, its value comes from the trust and confidence that people have in the issuing government. The term "fiat" is derived from the Latin word meaning "let it be done," indicating that the money is established by government order.
- **Legal Tender:** Fiat money is recognized by law as an acceptable form of payment for all debts, public and private. Governments enforce its use through legal tender laws, requiring it to be accepted for transactions within their jurisdictions.

Characteristics:

- **No Intrinsic Value:** Fiat money has value because the government maintains it and people have confidence in its stability.

- **Unlimited Supply:** Unlike commodity money, which is limited by the availability of the commodity (e.g., gold), fiat money can be produced in any amount by the issuing authority.

Historical Context:

Centralized Control: Central banks control the supply of fiat money, using monetary policy tools to manage inflation, interest rates, and economic stability.

Gold Standard: Before fiat money, many countries used the gold standard, where the value of currency was directly linked to a specific amount of gold. People could exchange banknotes for gold on demand, providing a tangible backing for the currency.

Abandonment of the Gold Standard: In the 20th century, the constraints of the gold standard became apparent, especially during times of economic crisis. The ability to adjust the money supply was limited by the availability of gold. The Great Depression and the two World Wars highlighted the need for more flexible monetary systems.

Bretton Woods System: After World War II, the Bretton Woods Agreement established a system where currencies were pegged to the US dollar, which was convertible to gold. This system lasted until 1971 when the US suspended the convertibility of the dollar to gold, marking the end of the gold standard and the beginning of the fiat currency era.

Advantages of Fiat Money:

- **Flexibility in Monetary Policy:** Central banks can control the money supply to manage economic variables such as inflation, interest rates, and unemployment. This flexibility allows for more responsive and proactive economic management.
- **Economic Stability:** By adjusting the money supply, governments can mitigate the effects of economic cycles, smoothing out recessions and curbing inflation.
- **Resource Allocation:** Fiat money does not tie up valuable resources like gold or silver, allowing them to be used for industrial and technological purposes instead of monetary backing.
- **Simplicity:** Fiat money simplifies the monetary system, making transactions and accounting more straightforward.

Disadvantages of Fiat Money:

- **Inflation Risk:** Because fiat money can be printed in unlimited quantities, there is a risk of inflation if too much money is introduced into the economy. Hyperinflation can erode the value of currency, leading to economic instability.
- **Loss of Intrinsic Value:** Fiat money relies entirely on trust and government backing. If confidence in the issuing authority diminishes, the value of the

currency can collapse, as seen in historical cases like the hyperinflation in Zimbabwe.
- **Centralized Control:** The power to control the money supply is concentrated in central banks, which can lead to concerns about transparency and accountability. Poor monetary policy decisions can have widespread negative effects.

Modern Use and Implications:

- **Global Standard:** Today, fiat money is the standard for most of the world's economies. Central banks, such as the Federal Reserve in the US and the European Central Bank, play crucial roles in managing the supply of money and ensuring economic stability.
- **Digital Age:** The rise of digital payment systems and cryptocurrencies has introduced new dynamics to the monetary landscape. While fiat money remains dominant, digital currencies present challenges and opportunities for future monetary systems.
- **Confidence and Trust:** The effectiveness of fiat money depends on the trust and confidence of the people who use it. Governments and central banks must maintain this trust through sound economic policies, transparency, and effective regulation.

In conclusion, fiat money represents a modern and flexible approach to monetary systems, allowing for more dynamic management of economies. Its success relies heavily on public trust and effective governance, highlighting the importance of responsible economic policies.

It's fascinating how we've moved from gold to paper, and now to digital currencies

Digital and Cryptocurrencies

The advent of the internet brought digital payment systems, and the 21st century saw the rise of cryptocurrencies like Bitcoin. These decentralized digital currencies use blockchain technology, challenging traditional financial systems and offering new possibilities for secure, transparent transactions.

In the rapidly evolving financial landscape, digital and cryptocurrencies have emerged as revolutionary forms of money, challenging traditional banking systems and reshaping how we perceive and use currency. Here's an in-depth look:

Digital Currencies:

Definition and Characteristics:

Digital Currency: Digital currency refers to any form of currency that is available only in digital or electronic form, unlike physical cash. This includes cryptocurrencies as well as centralized digital currencies issued by financial institutions.

Types: Digital currencies can be broadly classified into two categories: centralized digital currencies (such as those managed by banks or payment providers) and decentralized cryptocurrencies.

Examples:

Centralized Digital Currencies: Examples include digital payments via credit and debit cards, PayPal, and other online payment platforms. These systems are backed by traditional banks and financial institutions.

Central Bank Digital Currencies (CBDCs): Several countries are exploring or implementing CBDCs, which are digital versions of their national currencies. For instance, China has launched the digital yuan, and other countries like Sweden and the Bahamas are piloting their own versions.

Advantages:

- **Convenience:** Digital currencies offer ease of use, allowing for quick and seamless transactions online and in-store.
- **Global Reach:** They facilitate cross-border transactions, making international trade and remittances faster and more efficient.

- **Reduced Costs:** Digital payments can reduce transaction fees compared to traditional banking methods.
- **Transparency and Security:** Digital transactions leave an electronic trail, which can enhance transparency and reduce fraud.

Disadvantages:

- **Digital Divide:** Access to digital currencies requires technology and internet connectivity, which can be a barrier for underserved populations.
- **Cybersecurity Risks:** Digital currencies are vulnerable to hacking and cyber-attacks, posing a significant risk to users.
- **Privacy Concerns:** Centralized digital currencies can raise concerns about data privacy and government surveillance.

Cryptocurrencies:

Definition and Characteristics:

Cryptocurrency: Cryptocurrencies are decentralized digital currencies that use cryptographic techniques to secure transactions and control the creation of new units. They operate on blockchain technology, a distributed ledger that records all transactions transparently and immutably.

Decentralization: Unlike traditional currencies, cryptocurrencies are not controlled by any central authority, such as a government or bank. Instead, they rely on a decentralized network of computers (nodes) to validate and record transactions.

Examples:

Bitcoin: Launched in 2009 by an anonymous person or group known as Satoshi Nakamoto, Bitcoin is the first and most well-known cryptocurrency. It serves as a digital store of value and a medium of exchange.

Ethereum: Introduced in 2015, Ethereum is a blockchain platform that enables the creation of smart contracts and decentralized applications (DApps). Its native currency, Ether (ETH), powers the network.

Other Cryptocurrencies: There are thousands of other cryptocurrencies, including Litecoin, Ripple (XRP), Cardano, and Solana, each with unique features and use cases.

Advantages:

- **Decentralization:** Cryptocurrencies are not subject to government or institutional control, offering greater autonomy to users.
- **Security:** Blockchain technology provides a high level of security, making it difficult to alter transaction records or counterfeit currencies.
- **Transparency:** All transactions are recorded on a public ledger, promoting transparency and trust within the network.
- **Lower Transaction Fees:** Cryptocurrencies can reduce transaction costs, especially for cross-border payments.

Disadvantages:

- **Volatility:** Cryptocurrencies are known for their price volatility, which can pose significant risks to investors and users.
- **Regulatory Uncertainty:** The legal and regulatory environment for cryptocurrencies is still evolving, leading to uncertainty and potential legal challenges.
- **Scalability Issues:** Some cryptocurrencies face challenges in scaling their networks to handle large volumes of transactions efficiently.
- **Environmental Concerns:** The energy-intensive process of mining cryptocurrencies, particularly Bitcoin, raises environmental concerns due to high electricity consumption.

Impact on Economy and Society:

Financial Inclusion: Cryptocurrencies and digital currencies can promote financial inclusion by providing access to financial services for unbanked and underbanked populations.

Innovation and Development: The rise of cryptocurrencies has spurred innovation in various fields, including finance, technology, and supply chain management. Blockchain technology, in particular, has potential applications beyond currency, such as in voting systems, healthcare, and intellectual property.

Challenges to Traditional Banking: Cryptocurrencies pose a challenge to traditional banking systems by offering alternative means of storing and transferring value. Banks and financial institutions are exploring ways to integrate blockchain technology and digital assets into their services.

Speculation and Investment: Cryptocurrencies have become popular investment assets, attracting both individual and institutional investors. However, their speculative nature and price volatility can lead to significant financial risks.

Future Prospects:

Adoption and Regulation: The future of digital and cryptocurrencies will depend on their adoption by consumers and businesses, as well as the regulatory frameworks developed by governments worldwide.

Technological Advancements: Continued technological advancements in blockchain and related technologies will shape the evolution and capabilities of digital currencies.

Integration with Traditional Finance: The integration of digital and cryptocurrencies with traditional financial systems will create new opportunities and challenges for the global economy.

Digital and cryptocurrencies represent a transformative shift in the way we understand and use money. They offer numerous benefits, including convenience, security, and financial inclusion, but also pose challenges related to regulation, volatility, and technology. The ongoing evolution of these currencies will likely have profound implications for the future of finance and our global economy

Historical Figures and Their Views on Money:

Throughout history, many influential figures have shared their thoughts on money, its value, and its role in society. Here are a few notable examples:

1. Aristotle (384–322 BCE)

Aristotle, the ancient Greek philosopher, had a profound impact on economic thought. He distinguished between "use value" and "exchange value." According to Aristotle, money should have intrinsic value, meaning it should be something useful in itself, like gold or silver. He believed that money should facilitate trade without altering the value of goods.

2. Adam Smith (1723–1790)

Adam Smith, often referred to as the father of modern economics, wrote extensively about money in his seminal work, "The Wealth of Nations." Smith argued that money's primary function is to serve as a medium of exchange, facilitating trade and economic growth. He emphasized the importance of a stable currency and the dangers of inflation.

3. John Maynard Keynes (1883–1946)

John Maynard Keynes, a British economist, revolutionized economic theory with his ideas on government intervention in the economy. Keynes believed that money should be managed by the state to stabilize the economy. He advocated for fiscal and monetary policies to control inflation and unemployment, emphasizing the role of government in regulating the money supply.

4. Karl Marx (1818–1883)

Karl Marx, the German philosopher and economist, critiqued the capitalist system in his work, "Das Kapital." Marx viewed money as a representation of labor and argued that it was a tool used by capitalists to exploit workers. He believed that the value of money was derived from the labor required to produce goods and services.

5. Benjamin Franklin (1706–1790)

Benjamin Franklin, one of the Founding Fathers of the United States, had practical views on money. He emphasized the importance of thrift, hard work, and financial prudence. Franklin's famous adage, "A penny saved is a penny earned," reflects his belief in the value of saving and managing money wisely.

6. Milton Friedman (1912–2006)

Milton Friedman, an American economist, was a strong advocate for free-market capitalism. He believed that the best way to manage the economy was through controlling the money supply. Friedman argued that inflation was primarily a monetary phenomenon and that central banks should focus on maintaining stable prices.

7. Satoshi Nakamoto (Pseudonymous)

Satoshi Nakamoto, the mysterious creator of Bitcoin, introduced the concept of decentralized digital currency. Nakamoto's vision was to create a peer-to-peer electronic cash system that would eliminate the need for traditional financial intermediaries. Bitcoin and other cryptocurrencies have since challenged conventional notions of money and financial systems.

These historical figures have shaped our understanding of money and its role in society. Their ideas continue to influence economic thought and policy today

III. Money as an Essential Lifeline

Role in Trade and Commerce:

1. Medium of Exchange: Money acts as a standardized medium of exchange, simplifying the process of buying and selling goods and services. Without money, trade would rely on bartering, which requires a double coincidence of wants—where each party must have what the other wants. Money eliminates this complexity by providing a universally accepted means of payment.

2. Standard of Value: Money serves as a common measure of value, allowing for the easy comparison of prices across different goods and services. This standardization helps consumers make informed decisions, businesses to set prices, and markets to operate efficiently.

3. Store of Value: Money can be saved and stored over time, maintaining its value and enabling individuals and businesses to plan for the future. This ability to store wealth encourages saving and investment, which are crucial for economic growth and stability.

4. Facilitation of Trade: Money enables the efficient exchange of goods and services across long distances and different markets. It breaks down barriers to trade, allowing for the specialization of production and the benefits of economies of scale. With money, businesses can expand their reach beyond local markets to national and international levels.

5. Creation of Markets: Money helps create and sustain markets by providing liquidity. It allows buyers and sellers to engage in transactions quickly and easily, fostering competition and driving innovation. Markets, in turn, provide a mechanism for the allocation of resources, ensuring that goods and services are directed to where they are needed most.

6. Financial Instruments: Money underpins the creation of financial instruments such as bonds, stocks, and derivatives. These instruments facilitate investment, risk management, and capital formation, contributing to the growth and dynamism of the economy. Financial markets, powered by money, enable businesses to raise funds for expansion and innovation.

7. Economic Stability: By providing a stable and predictable means of payment, money contributes to economic stability. Central banks and monetary authorities manage the money supply to control inflation, stabilize prices, and promote full employment. A stable currency fosters confidence in the economy and encourages investment and consumption.

8. Consumer Confidence: A stable and widely accepted currency boosts consumer confidence. People are more willing to engage in economic activities, such as spending and investing, when they trust that the money they use will retain its value. This confidence is essential for the smooth functioning of commerce and the overall economy.

In essence, money is the lifeblood of trade and commerce. It facilitates transactions, provides a measure of value, stores wealth, and underpins financial systems. Its role in enabling efficient and widespread trade is fundamental to economic growth, innovation, and prosperity.

Providing Security and Stability:

1. Meeting Basic Needs: Money ensures that individuals and families can meet their essential needs such as food, shelter, clothing, and healthcare. Having sufficient financial resources means that people can afford necessities, which is foundational for a secure and stable life. This security alleviates anxiety about immediate survival and allows for a focus on longer-term goals and aspirations.

2. Emergency Preparedness: Financial stability provides a buffer against unexpected events and emergencies. Whether it's a sudden illness, job loss, or natural disaster, having savings and access to financial resources allows individuals to navigate crises without falling into severe hardship. This preparedness is crucial for maintaining stability in the face of life's uncertainties.

3. Access to Healthcare: With money, people can afford quality healthcare services, including routine check-ups, emergency treatments, and long-term care. Financial resources ensure that individuals can access medical treatments and medications when needed, contributing to overall well-being and longevity. Health security is a critical aspect of personal and familial stability.

4. Education and Skill Development: Money facilitates access to education and skill development opportunities. Whether it's primary education, higher education, or vocational training, financial resources enable individuals to invest in their futures. Education not only enhances personal growth but also improves job prospects and earning potential, leading to economic stability.

5. Retirement Planning: Financial stability allows for effective retirement planning. By saving and investing wisely, individuals can ensure that they have sufficient resources to maintain their lifestyle and cover expenses after they stop working. A well-planned retirement offers peace of mind and long-term security.

6. Financial Planning and Risk Management: Having money enables individuals to engage in financial planning and risk management. They can invest in insurance policies, diversify investments, and create emergency funds to safeguard against potential risks. This proactive approach to managing finances enhances stability and reduces vulnerability to economic fluctuations.

7. Housing Stability: Financial resources are essential for securing stable housing. Whether renting or buying a home, money ensures that individuals have a safe and comfortable place to live. Housing stability is foundational for personal security and well-being, providing a stable environment for families to thrive.

8. Social Mobility and Opportunity: Money provides the means for social mobility and access to opportunities. It enables individuals to pursue career advancements, entrepreneurial ventures, and new experiences. Financial resources open doors to personal and professional growth, fostering a sense of security and purpose.

9. Economic Stability: On a larger scale, financial stability contributes to overall economic stability. When individuals and families are financially secure, they are more likely to participate in the economy through spending, saving, and investing. This participation drives economic growth and stability, benefiting society as a whole.

In essence, money as an essential lifeline, provides the security and stability needed for individuals and families to lead fulfilling lives. It enables people to meet basic needs, plan for the future, navigate emergencies, and access opportunities for growth and development. Financial stability is a cornerstone of personal well-being and societal prosperity

Facilitating Personal Freedom and Empowerment:

1. Autonomy and Choice: Money provides individuals with the autonomy to make their own choices and decisions. With financial resources, people can determine how to spend their time, pursue their interests, and shape their lives according to their values and aspirations. This autonomy is a crucial aspect of personal freedom.

2. Pursuit of Education and Self-Improvement: Money enables access to education and self-improvement opportunities. Whether it's enrolling in a degree program, attending workshops, or participating in online courses, financial resources allow individuals to invest in their personal and professional development. Education empowers people with knowledge and skills, enhancing their potential and opening new doors.

3. Entrepreneurship and Innovation: Financial resources provide the capital necessary to start and grow businesses. Money empowers aspiring entrepreneurs to turn their ideas into reality, fostering innovation and economic dynamism. By investing in their ventures, individuals can create jobs, drive economic growth, and contribute to their communities.

4. Travel and Exploration: With money, individuals can travel and explore the world, experiencing new cultures, environments, and perspectives. Travel broadens horizons, enriches personal experiences, and fosters a sense of connection with the global community. Financial freedom allows people to embark on journeys that enhance their understanding of the world and themselves.

5. Personal Fulfillment and Hobbies: Money enables individuals to engage in hobbies and activities that bring them joy and fulfillment. Whether it's pursuing artistic endeavors, participating in sports, or enjoying leisure activities, financial resources provide the means to explore and nurture personal passions. This contributes to overall well-being and life satisfaction.

6. Health and Wellness: Financial resources allow individuals to invest in their health and wellness. This includes accessing quality healthcare, engaging in fitness activities, and maintaining a balanced diet. Money provides the freedom to prioritize and care for one's physical and mental well-being, leading to a healthier and more fulfilling life.

7. Social Mobility: Money plays a significant role in social mobility, allowing individuals to improve their socioeconomic status. Financial resources enable people to access better education, housing, and employment opportunities, breaking the cycle of poverty and creating pathways to success. This empowerment is essential for achieving equality and justice.

8. Financial Independence: Achieving financial independence means having sufficient resources to support oneself without relying on others. This independence provides a sense of security and confidence, freeing individuals from financial constraints and dependencies. It empowers people to live on their own terms and make decisions that align with their goals.

9. Impact and Philanthropy: Money provides the means to make a positive impact on society through philanthropy and charitable giving. Individuals with financial resources can support causes they care about, contribute to social initiatives, and help those in need. This ability to give back and make a difference empowers individuals to create meaningful change.

10. Planning and Stability: Financial resources allow individuals to plan for the future, ensuring stability and security. Whether it's saving for retirement, investing in long-term goals, or creating an emergency fund, money provides the foundation for a stable and secure life. This planning and foresight contribute to personal empowerment and peace of mind.

In essence, money as an essential lifeline facilitates personal freedom and empowerment by providing the means to pursue education, entrepreneurship, travel, hobbies, health, and social mobility. It enables individuals to make choices that align with their values and goals, leading to a more fulfilling and autonomous life

Economic Growth and Development:

1. Investment and Capital Formation: Money is fundamental to investment and capital formation, which are the cornerstones of economic growth. Individuals and businesses save and accumulate money, which is then invested in various ventures such as new businesses, infrastructure projects, and technological innovations. These investments drive economic expansion, create jobs, and foster development.

2. Innovation and Entrepreneurship: Financial resources enable entrepreneurs to develop new products and services, enhancing innovation and competitiveness. Money provides the capital necessary for research and development, allowing businesses to bring cutting-edge technologies and ideas to market. This process not only drives economic growth but also improves the quality of life by introducing better and more efficient solutions.

3. Infrastructure Development: Government and private investments in infrastructure—such as roads, bridges, airports, and utilities—are crucial for economic development. Money finances these projects, which in turn facilitate trade, improve connectivity, and support the efficient movement of goods and people. Robust infrastructure is essential for a thriving economy, reducing costs, and boosting productivity.

4. Financial Markets: Money fuels financial markets, where stocks, bonds, and other financial instruments are traded.

These markets provide companies with access to capital needed for expansion and innovation. Financial markets also offer investment opportunities for individuals, promoting wealth accumulation and economic stability.

5. Consumption and Demand: Consumer spending is a major driver of economic growth. Money in the hands of consumers translates into demand for goods and services. This demand encourages businesses to produce more, leading to higher employment rates and income levels. The cycle of spending and production creates a positive feedback loop that sustains economic growth.

6. Government Expenditures: Governments rely on money to fund public services and social programs such as healthcare, education, and social security. Public spending on these services improves the well-being of citizens, enhances human capital, and supports long-term economic development. Additionally, government investments in infrastructure and technology can stimulate economic activity.

7. International Trade: Money facilitates international trade by enabling the exchange of goods and services between countries. Currencies act as a medium of exchange in global markets, allowing countries to specialize in the production of goods where they have a comparative advantage. This specialization leads to more efficient resource allocation, increased productivity, and economic growth.

8. Savings and Stability: Savings provide a safety net for individuals and contribute to financial stability. When people save money, it can be lent out by banks to fund various economic activities. These savings are crucial for long-term investments and help cushion the economy against shocks. A high savings rate can lead to lower interest rates, encouraging borrowing and investment.

9. Education and Human Capital: Investing in education and skills development is essential for economic growth. Money allocated to education ensures that individuals are equipped with the knowledge and skills needed to participate in the economy. A well-educated workforce attracts businesses and fosters innovation, driving long-term economic development.

10. Poverty Reduction and Social Progress: Economic growth fueled by money can lead to poverty reduction and social progress. By creating jobs and increasing incomes, economic development can lift people out of poverty and improve living standards. Financial resources also enable the provision of social services, reducing inequality and promoting inclusive growth.

In conclusion, money is a vital lifeline for economic growth and development. It enables investment, fosters innovation, supports infrastructure projects, drives consumer demand, and facilitates international trade. By providing the resources needed for various economic activities, money underpins the complex web of interactions that sustain and enhance economies. Understanding the multifaceted role of money in economic growth is key to devising policies that promote sustainable development and prosperity

IV. Money as a Necessary Evil

Moral and ethical concerns

Money is a paradox. It's the driving force behind economies, yet it can also lead to the downfall of moral and ethical principles. The concept of money as a necessary evil touch upon its essential role in society, but also highlights its potential to corrupt and divide. Let's dive into this complex relationship by examining both its indispensable utility and the moral quandaries it introduces.

The Role of Money in Society

At its core, money is a tool that facilitates trade and economic growth. It allows for the efficient exchange of goods and services, measures value, and incentivizes innovation. Without money, modern economies and civilizations would struggle to function. It's the lubricant that keeps the wheels of commerce turning, making it a necessary component of daily life.

However, the necessity of money comes with a price. The very nature of money often places a value on aspects of life that should remain priceless. Human dignity, health, happiness, and the environment are often overshadowed by the pursuit of wealth. This leads to a host of moral and ethical concerns that must be addressed.

Moral Concerns

Money's influence on human behavior is profound. On a moral level, the pursuit of wealth can lead individuals to compromise their integrity and values. This is evident in various unethical practices, such as exploitation, environmental degradation, and corruption.

Exploitation

The relentless drive for profit can result in the exploitation of workers and resources. Sweatshops, child labor, and unfair wages are all manifestations of this moral compromise. Companies prioritize their bottom line, often at the expense of human welfare. This exploitation is not just confined to distant factories but can be seen in various industries worldwide.

Environmental Degradation

The quest for economic growth often leads to environmental harm. Industries extract natural resources without regard for sustainability, leading to deforestation, pollution, and climate change. The moral cost of prioritizing short-term profits over long-term environmental health is immense. This disregard for the environment reflects a broader ethical failure to respect the intrinsic value of nature.

Corruption

Money has the power to corrupt even the most virtuous individuals. The desire for wealth can lead to dishonest behavior, from bribery and embezzlement to outright fraud.

Corruption undermines trust in institutions and erodes the social fabric. It creates an uneven playing field where those with money can manipulate systems to their advantage, further perpetuating inequality.

Ethical Concerns

Beyond the moral failings, money raises significant ethical questions about justice, equity, and the distribution of resources.

Wealth Disparity

One of the most glaring ethical issues related to money is the stark disparity in wealth distribution. The concentration of wealth in the hands of a few creates a significant divide between the rich and the poor. This disparity fosters social unrest and erodes the sense of community. It raises fundamental questions about justice: why should a small percentage of the population control a vast majority of the resources while many lack accesses to basic necessities?

Inherited Wealth and Systemic Inequalities

Inherited wealth and systemic inequalities perpetuate a cycle where the rich get richer, and the poor struggle to improve their circumstances. This inequity can be seen in access to education, healthcare, and opportunities. Money, or the lack thereof, often determines one's fate. This perpetuation of inequality challenges our ethical notions of fairness and meritocracy.

Access to Opportunities

Ethically, the distribution of money impacts access to opportunities. Those with wealth have greater access to quality education, healthcare, and career prospects. This creates an uneven playing field where the underprivileged are left at a disadvantage from the start. The ethical implications of such inequality challenge the very foundations of a just society

Income Inequality:

A Growing Concern

Income inequality refers to the unequal distribution of wealth and income among individuals and groups within a society. This inequality manifests in various forms, including disparities in wages, access to education, healthcare, and opportunities for advancement. The concentration of wealth in the hands of a few creates a significant divide between the affluent and the impoverished, with far-reaching consequences.

Wealth Concentration

One of the most visible aspects of income inequality is the concentration of wealth. A small percentage of the population controls a large portion of the world's resources, leaving the majority with limited means. This concentration of wealth is often perpetuated through mechanisms such as inheritance, investment opportunities, and access to superior education and healthcare.

The wealthy have the means to invest in lucrative ventures, secure higher returns, and accumulate more assets. This creates a self-reinforcing cycle where the rich get richer, while the poor struggle to make ends meet. Such disparities are not just confined to individual countries; they are evident on a global scale, with significant differences between developed and developing nations.

Access to Education and Opportunities

Income inequality also impacts access to education and opportunities. Wealthier families can afford to send their children to prestigious schools, providing them with a significant advantage in terms of knowledge, skills, and networking. This educational disparity translates into differences in career prospects and earning potential, perpetuating the cycle of inequality.

On the other hand, individuals from lower-income backgrounds often face numerous barriers to accessing quality education. Underfunded schools, lack of resources, and socio-economic challenges hinder their ability to compete on an equal footing. This results in limited opportunities for social mobility and a persistent gap between the rich and the poor.

Health Disparities

Income inequality extends to healthcare, with wealthier individuals enjoying better access to medical services, nutrition, and overall well-being. Higher-income groups can afford private healthcare, regular check-ups, and a healthier lifestyle, leading to longer life expectancy and better health outcomes. In contrast, those with lower incomes often rely on underfunded public healthcare systems, struggle with medical expenses, and face higher rates of illness and mortality.

The ethical implications of such disparities are profound. Health should be a fundamental human right, yet income inequality creates a situation where access to healthcare is determined by one's financial status. This not only undermines the principles of equity and justice but also exacerbates societal divisions.

Societal Divide: Consequences of Income Inequality

The societal divide created by income inequality has far-reaching implications for social cohesion, trust, and overall stability. When wealth is concentrated in the hands of a few, it leads to a breakdown in the social fabric, fostering resentment, alienation, and social unrest.

Social Cohesion and Trust

Income inequality erodes social cohesion by creating distinct socio-economic classes that operate in separate spheres. The wealthy live in affluent neighborhoods, attend prestigious institutions, and interact within exclusive social circles. Meanwhile, the poor reside in marginalized areas, attend underfunded schools, and face daily struggles to make ends meet. This segregation limits interactions between different socio-economic groups, leading to a lack of understanding and empathy.

Moreover, income inequality undermines trust in institutions and society as a whole. When people perceive the system as unjust and rigged in favor of the wealthy, it erodes their faith in governance, legal systems, and social structures. This lack of trust can lead to disillusionment, disengagement, and a sense of powerlessness, further deepening the societal divide.

Resentment and Social Unrest

The visible disparity between the rich and the poor often breeds resentment and social unrest. When individuals feel that their efforts go unrewarded and that opportunities for upward mobility are limited, it can lead to frustration and anger. This discontent can manifest in various forms, including protests, strikes, and even violence.

Historical events have shown that extreme income inequality can destabilize societies and

lead to revolutions. The French Revolution, for instance, was driven in part by widespread poverty and the concentration of wealth among the aristocracy. Similarly, contemporary movements like the Occupy Wall Street protests highlight the ongoing struggle against economic disparities and the demand for greater equality.

The Ethical Dimension of Money and Inequality

The existence of income inequality raises profound ethical questions about justice, fairness, and the distribution of resources. It challenges the moral fabric of society, questioning whether it is justifiable for some to live in opulence while others struggle for survival.

Fairness and Justice

At the heart of the ethical debate is the question of fairness. Should individuals born into wealth have an inherent advantage over those born into poverty? Should access to education, healthcare, and opportunities be determined by one's financial status? These questions strike at the core of ethical principles, challenging the notion of a just and equitable society.

Fairness implies that everyone should have an equal opportunity to succeed, regardless of their background. However, income inequality perpetuates a system where success is often determined by factors beyond one's control, such as family wealth and social connections. This undermines the meritocratic ideals that many societies aspire to uphold.

Distribution of Resources

The ethical implications of income inequality also extend to the distribution of resources. Wealthier individuals and corporations often have disproportionate influence over political and economic systems, shaping policies that benefit their interests. This concentration of power can result in tax policies, labor laws, and regulations that further entrench inequality, perpetuating a cycle of privilege and disadvantage.

Moreover, the unequal distribution of resources raises questions about the ethical responsibilities of the wealthy. Should those with vast resources have a moral obligation to contribute to the welfare of society? The concept of philanthropy and corporate social responsibility reflects an acknowledgment of this duty, but it is often limited and voluntary, falling short of addressing systemic inequalities

Stress and Mental Health Implications

Money plays a pivotal role in our lives, shaping opportunities, lifestyles, and even our sense of self-worth. While it is indispensable for facilitating economic transactions and driving growth, its pervasive influence also brings about significant stress and mental health implications.

The Psychological Burden of Financial Stress

Financial stress is a pervasive issue that affects individuals across all socioeconomic backgrounds. The constant need to manage finances, meet expenses, and plan for the future can be overwhelming and lead to significant psychological distress.

Anxiety and Depression

Financial instability is a major source of anxiety and depression. The uncertainty of not knowing whether one can meet basic needs, pay bills, or save for the future can create a constant state of worry. This anxiety can manifest in various ways, including sleep disturbances, irritability, and difficulty concentrating. Over time, chronic financial stress can lead to more severe mental health issues, such as depression.

Depression related to financial stress often stems from feelings of helplessness and despair. Individuals may feel trapped in their circumstances, with no clear path to financial security. This sense of hopelessness can lead to withdrawal from social activities, decreased motivation, and even suicidal thoughts.

Relationship Strain

Money issues are a leading cause of relationship problems. Financial stress can strain relationships, leading to arguments, resentment, and a breakdown in communication. Couples may disagree on spending priorities, debt management, and financial goals. These conflicts can erode trust and intimacy, ultimately impacting the overall quality of the relationship.

Social Isolation

Financial stress can also lead to social isolation. Individuals who are struggling financially may feel embarrassed or ashamed of their situation, leading them to withdraw from social interactions. They may avoid activities that require spending money or feel uncomfortable discussing their financial challenges with friends and family. This isolation can exacerbate feelings of loneliness and depression.

The Impact of Debt on Mental Health

Debt is a significant contributor to financial stress and its associated mental health issues. The burden of debt can feel insurmountable, leading to a constant state of anxiety and fear. The pressure to meet debt obligations can create a cycle of stress that is difficult to break.

The Debt Spiral

The debt spiral occurs when individuals take on more debt to manage existing debt, leading to a never-ending cycle of financial strain. High-interest rates and fees can make it nearly impossible to pay down the principal amount, trapping individuals in a cycle of debt. This situation can lead to feelings of hopelessness and despair, as individuals struggle to see a way out.

Shame and Guilt

Debt can also lead to feelings of shame and guilt. Individuals may feel that their debt is a reflection of personal failure or poor financial management. This shame can prevent them from seeking help or discussing their situation with others, further exacerbating their stress and isolation.

The Societal Pressure to Achieve Financial Success

Society often equates financial success with personal worth, creating immense pressure to achieve monetary milestones. This pressure can lead to unhealthy behaviors and mental health challenges.

Materialism and Consumerism

The pervasive culture of materialism and consumerism can create unrealistic expectations and drive individuals to pursue wealth at all costs. Advertising and social media often portray an idealized version of life, where happiness and success are measured by material possessions. This constant bombardment can lead to a relentless pursuit of money and status, often at the expense of mental well-being.

Fear of Failure

The fear of financial failure can be debilitating. The pressure to succeed financially can lead to perfectionism, risk-aversion, and an overwhelming fear of making mistakes. This fear can stifle creativity and innovation, as individuals become preoccupied with avoiding financial setbacks.

The Role of Economic Inequality

Economic inequality further compounds the mental health implications of money. The disparity between the rich and the poor can create a sense of injustice and hopelessness, particularly for those who feel trapped in poverty.

The Psychological Impact of Inequality

Economic inequality can lead to feelings of inadequacy, resentment, and social comparison. Individuals who perceive themselves as being less successful or less wealthy than others may experience lower self-esteem and increased stress. This constant comparison can create a sense of inadequacy and drive individuals to engage in unhealthy behaviors in an attempt to keep up.

Limited Access to Mental Health Resources

Economic inequality also impacts access to mental health resources. Those with limited financial means may struggle to afford therapy, medication, or other forms of mental health support. This lack of access can exacerbate mental health issues and prevent individuals from seeking the help they need.

Corruption and Crime

The indispensability of money does not come without a cost. Its omnipresence in our lives creates opportunities for misuse and exploitation, leading to significant corruption and criminal activities.

Corruption: The Dark Side of Wealth

Corruption involves the abuse of power for personal gain, often facilitated by money. It is a pervasive issue that affects all levels of society, from local government officials to international corporations. Corruption undermines trust, erodes institutions, and perpetuates inequality.

Political Corruption

Political corruption is one of the most damaging forms of corruption. It involves the misuse of public office for private benefit, often through bribery, embezzlement, and nepotism. Politicians and public officials may exploit their positions to secure financial advantages, undermining the principles of democracy and good governance.

Bribery is a common manifestation of political corruption. It occurs when individuals or businesses offer money or gifts to public officials in exchange for favorable treatment, contracts, or policy decisions. This practice not only distorts the allocation of resources but also erodes public trust in government institutions.

Embezzlement is another prevalent form of political corruption. Public officials may siphon off public funds for personal use, depriving citizens of essential services and infrastructure. This misappropriation of resources hampers development efforts and exacerbates poverty and inequality.

Nepotism and favoritism further contribute to political corruption. Public officials may appoint friends, family members, or loyal supporters to positions of power, regardless of their qualifications. This practice undermines meritocracy and perpetuates inefficiency and incompetence within public institutions.

Corporate Corruption

Corporate corruption involves unethical behavior by businesses and their executives to secure financial gain. This can include practices such as fraud, insider trading, tax evasion, and bribery of foreign officials. Corporate corruption distorts markets, undermines fair competition, and damages the reputation of legitimate businesses.

Fraud is a common form of corporate corruption. It involves deceptive practices intended to secure unfair or unlawful financial gain. This can include falsifying financial statements, manipulating stock prices, and engaging in Ponzi schemes. Corporate fraud not only harms investors and stakeholders but also undermines the integrity of financial markets.

Insider trading is another prevalent issue in the corporate world. It occurs when individuals with access to non-public information about a company use that information to make profitable stock trades. Insider trading undermines investor confidence and creates an uneven playing field, as those with privileged information can unfairly profit at the expense of others.

Tax evasion is a significant problem in both the public and private sectors. Corporations and wealthy individuals may use complex schemes to hide income and assets, avoiding their fair share of taxes. This practice deprives governments of revenue needed for public services and infrastructure, exacerbating inequality and undermining social cohesion.

Crime: The Pursuit of Illicit Wealth

Money is often at the root of criminal activities, driving individuals and organized groups to engage in illegal behavior for financial gain. The pursuit of illicit wealth can take many forms,

from street-level crimes to sophisticated international operations.

Organized Crime

Organized crime refers to criminal activities carried out by structured groups that operate on a large scale. These groups engage in a range of illegal activities, including drug trafficking, human trafficking, money laundering, and extortion. Organized crime networks are driven by the pursuit of profit and often use violence and intimidation to achieve their goals.

Drug trafficking is one of the most lucrative forms of organized crime. Criminal organizations produce, transport, and distribute illegal drugs, generating enormous profits. This trade fuels addiction, violence, and social instability, with devastating consequences for communities and individuals.

Human trafficking is another heinous crime driven by the pursuit of money. Traffickers exploit vulnerable individuals, forcing them into labor or sexual exploitation. Human trafficking is a gross violation of human rights and dignity, and its profits fund further criminal activities.

Money Laundering

Money laundering is a critical component of organized crime. It involves disguising the origins of illegally obtained money to make it appear legitimate. Money laundering allows criminals to enjoy the proceeds

The Process of Money Laundering

Money laundering typically involves three stages: placement, layering, and integration.

Placement is the initial stage where illicit money is introduced into the financial system. This can be done through various means such as depositing small amounts into bank accounts, purchasing high-value assets like real estate or luxury goods, or using casinos and other cash- intensive businesses.

Layering involves a series of transactions designed to obscure the origin of the money. This stage often includes transferring funds between multiple accounts, sometimes across different countries, using shell companies, and engaging in complex financial transactions to make tracing the funds difficult. The aim is to disconnect the money from its illicit source.

Integration is the final stage, where the laundered money is integrated into the legitimate economy. At this point, the funds appear to be legitimate income or investment returns. This can be achieved through various means such as investing in businesses, purchasing luxury items, or converting the money into legitimate financial instruments like stocks or bonds.

Impact on Society

The impact of money laundering on society is profound and multifaceted. It enables organised crime groups to fund their operations, perpetuating a cycle of crime and corruption. This, in turn, undermines the rule of law and weakens institutions. Moreover, money laundering distorts economic data, making it difficult for governments and regulators to make informed decisions. It can also lead to unfair competition, as businesses associated with organised crime can outcompete legitimate enterprises by using laundered funds.

Furthermore, money laundering can facilitate other forms of corruption. For example, politicians or public officials may be bribed to ignore illegal activities or to protect criminal

enterprises. This undermines public trust in government and institutions, leading to a breakdown in social cohesion and stability.

Combating Money Laundering

Efforts to combat money laundering involve a combination of legal, regulatory, and enforcement measures. Governments and international organisations have implemented various frameworks to detect and prevent money laundering. These include stringent reporting requirements for financial institutions, cross-border cooperation and information sharing, and the establishment of specialised financial intelligence units.

One of the most significant international agreements in this regard is the Financial Action Task Force (FATF), which sets global standards for combating money laundering and terrorist financing. Compliance with FATF recommendations is essential for countries to effectively address the issue and protect their financial systems from abuse.

V. The Solution: Balancing & Finding Middle Ground

The solutions of balancing and finding a middle ground for better money management and financial literacy can be achieved in both Modern and Spiritual ways

Modern Ways: Money Management and Financial Literacy

Finding a middle ground in money management and financial literacy is all about balance. It involves managing your finances wisely while understanding the importance of financial knowledge to make informed decisions. Here's how you can strike that balance:

Understanding Financial Literacy

Financial literacy is the ability to understand and effectively use various financial skills, including personal financial management, budgeting, and investing. It's about knowing how money works, how to manage it, and how to grow it. It's essential because it helps you make informed decisions and avoid common pitfalls like debt and poor investment choices.

Money Management Basics

Budgeting: Creating a budget is the first step in effective money management. It helps you track your income and expenses, ensuring you live within your means. A good budget includes all sources of income and categorizes expenses into needs (rent, groceries) and wants (dining out, entertainment).

Saving: A crucial aspect of money management is saving. It's advisable to have an emergency fund that can cover at least three to six months of living expenses. Regular savings contribute to financial stability and prepare you for unforeseen expenses.

Investing: Investing is key to growing your wealth. Understanding different investment options like stocks, bonds, and real estate helps you diversify your portfolio and minimize risks. It's essential to start investing early to benefit from compound interest.

Debt Management: Managing debt effectively is critical. This includes understanding the difference between good debt (like a mortgage) and bad debt (like high-interest credit cards). Paying off high-interest debts first and avoiding unnecessary debt can save you money in the long run.

Striking the Balance

Education: Continuously educate yourself about financial matters. This can include reading books, taking courses, or consulting financial advisors. The more you know, the better decisions you can make.

Practical Application: Apply what you learn in real-life situations. Start small with budgeting and saving, then gradually move on to more complex financial tasks like investing.

Review and Adjust: Regularly review your financial plan and make adjustments as needed. Life circumstances change, and your financial plan should be flexible enough to accommodate these changes.

Key Tips

Set Financial Goals: Clear financial goals give you direction and motivation. Whether it's saving for a house, a car, or retirement, having specific targets helps you stay focused.

Live Below Your Means: This is a fundamental principle of financial stability. Spend less than you earn and avoid lifestyle inflation, which means increasing your spending as your income increases.

Use Technology: Leverage financial tools and apps that help with budgeting, saving, and investing. These tools can simplify money management and provide valuable insights

Spiritual Ways: Money Management and Financial Literacy

Integrating spirituality with money management and financial literacy involves viewing finances not just as a means to an end, but as a reflection of your values and a tool for fostering well- being. Here's how you can approach it:

Mindful Spending and Saving

Intentional Spending: Be deliberate about where your money goes. Spend on things that truly matter to you and align with your values. This helps you feel more content and less materialistic.

Gratitude and Contentment: Practice gratitude for what you already have. This reduces the desire for unnecessary expenditures and promotes a sense of contentment.

Spiritual Principles in Financial Planning

Simplicity: Embrace simplicity by focusing on needs over wants. Simplifying your life can lead to less stress and greater financial clarity.

Generosity: Sharing your wealth, whether through charity or helping others in need, can foster a sense of community and purpose. This aligns with many spiritual teachings that emphasize the importance of giving.

Ethical Investments: Invest in ways that align with your values, such as socially responsible or sustainable investments. This ensures that your money supports causes you believe in.

Holistic Financial Health

Balance and Harmony: Seek a balance between earning, saving, spending, and giving. This approach fosters harmony in your financial life and supports your overall well-being.

Long-Term Perspective: Adopt a long-term perspective on wealth, focusing on sustainability and legacy rather than immediate gratification.

Mindfulness Practices

Financial Meditation: Reflect on your financial goals and decisions regularly. Meditation can help you stay grounded and clear-minded when managing money.

Mindful Budgeting: Create and review your budget with a mindful approach. This involves being fully present and aware of your financial choices.

Continuous Learning and Growth

Spiritual Financial Education: Learn about money management from a perspective that incorporates spiritual and ethical principles. Books, courses, and workshops can provide valuable insights.

Self-Reflection: Regularly reflect on your financial habits and their alignment with your spiritual beliefs. This helps you stay true to your values and make necessary adjustments.

Community and Support

Supportive Networks: Engage with communities that share similar values. Discussing financial matters with like-minded individuals can provide support and new perspectives.

Mentorship and Guidance: Seek guidance from mentors who embody both financial wisdom and spiritual integrity. They can offer valuable advice and inspiration.

Integrating spirituality into your financial life is about finding a balance that nurtures both your material and spiritual well-being. By approaching money with mindfulness, intentionality, and ethical consideration, you can create a financial life that truly reflects your values

Bhagavad Gita: Detailed Insights on Money

The Bhagavad Gita, a 700-verse Hindu scripture that is part of the Indian epic Mahabharata, provides profound teachings on various aspects of life, including the role and perception of money. Although it doesn't explicitly discuss modern financial systems, its principles can be applied to understand how one should handle money and material wealth. Here are some key insights:

Detachment from Material Wealth

One of the central themes of the Gita is detachment (Vairagya). Lord Krishna advises Arjuna to perform his duties without attachment to the results. This concept can be applied to money management by focusing on earning and using money responsibly without becoming emotionally attached to it.

Verse Reference: In Chapter 2, Verse 47, Krishna says,

karmaṇy evādhikāras te mā phaleṣu kadācana

mā karma-phala-hetur bhūr mā te saṅgo 'stv akarmaṇi

Synonyms

karmaṇi — in prescribed duties; *eva* — certainly; *adhikāraḥ* — right; *te* — of you; *mā* — never; *phaleṣu* — in the fruits; *kadācana* — at any time; *mā* — never; *karma-phala* — in the result of the work; *hetuḥ* — cause; *bhūḥ* — become; *mā* — never; *te* — of you; *saṅgaḥ* — attachment; *astu* — there should be; *akarmaṇi* — in not doing prescribed duties.

"You have a right to perform your prescribed duty, but you are not entitled to the fruits of action. Never consider yourself the cause of the results of your activities, and never be attached to not doing your duty"

Application: This teaches us to focus on the effort we put into earning money, rather than obsessing over the wealth itself. By practicing detachment, we can reduce anxiety related to financial outcomes and make more balanced decisions.

Selfless Service (Nishkama Karma)

The Gita promotes the idea of selfless action, where one performs their duties for the benefit of society without selfish desires. This principle can be extended to financial decisions, emphasizing the importance of using wealth for the greater good.

Verse Reference: In Chapter 3, Verse 19, Krishna states, *tasmād asaktaḥ satataṁ*

kāryaṁ karma samācara

asakto hy ācaran karma

param āpnoti pūruṣaḥ

Synonyms

tasmāt — therefore; asaktaḥ — without attachment; satatam — constantly; kāryam — as duty; karma — work; samācara — perform; asaktaḥ — unattached; hi — certainly; ācaran — performing; karma — work; param — the Supreme; āpnoti — achieves; pūruṣaḥ — a man.

"Therefore, without being attached to the fruits of activities, one should act as a matter of duty, for by working without attachment one attains the Supreme."

Application: This encourages using a portion of one's earnings for charitable purposes, community development, and helping those in need. It aligns financial actions with spiritual growth and societal well-being.

Balance and Moderation

The Gita advocates for a balanced life, avoiding extremes. This includes how one handles money. It encourages moderation in spending, saving, and investing, promoting a sustainable and stress-free financial life.

Verse Reference: In Chapter 6, Verse 16-17, Krishna advises,

yuktāhāra-vihārasya

yukta-ceṣṭasya karmasu

yukta-svapnāvabodhasya

yogo bhavati duḥkha-hā

Synonyms

yukta — regulated; āhāra — eating; vihārasya — recreation; yukta — regulated; ceṣṭasya — of one who works for maintenance; karmasu — in discharging duties; yukta — regulated; svapna-avabodhasya — sleep and wakefulness; yogaḥ — practice of yoga; bhavati — becomes; duḥkha-hā — diminishing pains.

He who is regulated in his habits of eating, sleeping, recreation and work can mitigate all material pains by practicing the yoga system.

yadā viniyataṁ cittam

ātmany evāvatiṣṭhate

nispṛhaḥ sarva-kāmebhyo

yukta ity ucyate tadā

Synonyms

yadā — when; viniyatam — particularly disciplined; cittam — the mind and its activities; ātmani — in the transcendence; eva — certainly; avatiṣṭhate — becomes situated; nispṛhaḥ — devoid of desire; sarva — for all kinds of; kāmebhyaḥ — material sense gratification; yuktaḥ — well situated in yoga; iti — thus; ucyate — is said to be; tadā — at that time.

When the yogī, by practice of yoga, disciplines his mental activities and becomes situated in transcendence – devoid of all material desires – he is said to be well established in yoga.

"There is no possibility of one's becoming a yogi, O Arjuna, if one eats too much or eats too little, sleeps too much or does not sleep enough. He who is temperate in his habits of eating, sleeping, working, and recreation can mitigate all material pains by practicing the yoga system."

Application: This principle guides us to budget wisely, avoid excessive spending or hoarding, and find a middle path that ensures financial stability without compromising on life's joys and responsibilities.

Inner Fulfillment

The Gita teaches that true happiness and fulfillment come from within and are not dependent on external wealth or possessions. It encourages spiritual growth and inner peace as the foundation for a satisfying life.

Verse Reference: In Chapter 2, Verse 55, Krishna says,

śrī-bhagavān uvāca

prajahāti yadā kāmān

sarvān pārtha mano-gatān

ātmany evātmanā tuṣṭaḥ

sthita-prajñas tadocyate

Synonyms

śrī-bhagavān uvāca — the Supreme Personality of Godhead said; prajahāti — gives up; yadā — when; kāmān — desires for sense gratification; sarvān — of all varieties; pārtha — O son of Pṛthā; manaḥ-gatān — of mental concoction; ātmani — in the pure state of the soul; eva — certainly; ātmanā — by the purified mind; tuṣṭaḥ — satisfied; sthita-prajñaḥ — transcendentally situated; tadā — at that time; ucyate — is said.

"A person who is not disturbed by the incessant flow of desires—that enter like rivers into the ocean, which is ever being filled but is always still—can alone achieve peace, and not the man who strives to satisfy such desires."

Application: This principle reminds us to seek contentment and peace within ourselves rather than constantly chasing material wealth. It advocates for a simple life where financial goals are balanced with spiritual and personal growth.

Ethical Living

The Gita emphasizes righteousness (Dharma) and living a life of integrity and honesty. This includes earning money through ethical means and ensuring that financial dealings do not harm others.

Verse Reference: In Chapter 16, Verse 1-3, Krishna describes the qualities of a divine person, including fearlessness, purity of heart, self-discipline, and charity.

śrī-bhagavān uvāca

abhayaṁ sattva-saṁśuddhir

jñāna-yoga-vyavasthitiḥ

dānaṁ damaś ca yajñaś ca

svādhyāyas tapa ārjavam

ahiṁsā satyam akrodhas

tyāgaḥ śāntir apaiśunam

dayā bhūteṣv aloluptvaṁ

mārdavaṁ hrīr acāpalam

tejaḥ kṣamā dhṛtiḥ śaucam

adroho nāti-mānitā

bhavanti sampadaṁ daivīm

abhijātasya bhārata

Synonyms

śrī-bhagavān uvāca — the Supreme Personality of Godhead said; abhayam — fearlessness; sattva-saṁśuddhiḥ — purification of one's existence; jñāna — in knowledge; yoga — of linking up; vyavasthitiḥ — the situation; dānam — charity; damaḥ — controlling the mind; ca — and; yajñaḥ — performance of sacrifice; ca — and; svādhyāyaḥ — study of Vedic literature; tapaḥ — austerity; ārjavam — simplicity; ahiṁsā — nonviolence; satyam — truthfulness; akrodhaḥ — freedom from anger; tyāgaḥ — renunciation; śāntiḥ —

tranquillity; apaiśunam — aversion to fault-finding; dayā — mercy; bhūteṣu — towards all living entities; aloluptvam — freedom from greed; mārdavam — gentleness; hrīḥ — modesty; acāpalam — determination; tejaḥ — vigor; kṣamā — forgiveness; dhṛtiḥ — fortitude; śaucam — cleanliness; adrohaḥ — freedom from envy; na — not; ati-mānitā — expectation of honor; bhavanti — are; sampadam — the qualities; daivīm — the transcendental nature; abhijātasya — of one who is born of; bhārata — O son of Bharata.

The Supreme Personality of Godhead said: Fearlessness; purification of one's existence; cultivation of spiritual knowledge; charity; self-control; performance of sacrifice; study of the Vedas; austerity; simplicity; nonviolence; truthfulness; freedom from anger; renunciation; tranquillity; aversion to faultfinding; compassion for all living entities; freedom from covetousness; gentleness; modesty; steady determination; vigor; forgiveness; fortitude; cleanliness; and freedom from envy and from the passion for honor – these transcendental qualities, O son of Bharata, belong to godly men endowed with divine nature

Application: This encourages earning a livelihood through honest and ethical means, avoiding exploitation and ensuring fairness in all financial transactions. It promotes transparency and integrity in business practices.

Detachment and Equanimity

Krishna advises maintaining equanimity in success and failure, profit and loss. This mindset helps in managing financial stress and cultivates a balanced perspective on money.

Verse Reference: In Chapter 2, Verse 38, Krishna says,

sukha-duḥkhe same kṛtvā

lābhālābhau jayājayau

tato yuddhāya yujyasva

naivaṁ pāpam avāpsyasi

Synonyms

sukha — happiness; duḥkhe — and distress; same — in equanimity; kṛtvā — doing so; lābha-alābhau — both profit and loss; jaya-ajayau — both victory and defeat; tataḥ — thereafter; yuddhāya — for the sake of fighting; yujyasva — engage (fight); na — never; evam — in this way; pāpam — sinful reaction; avāpsyasi — you will gain

"Having made pleasure and pain, gain and loss, victory and defeat the same, engage in battle for the sake of battle; thus, you shall not incur sin."

Application: This encourages viewing financial ups and downs with a calm and balanced mind. It reduces the emotional impact of financial fluctuations and helps in making rational decisions without being swayed by fear or greed.

Integrating Gita's Teachings into Modern Financial Life

Mindful Financial Planning: Use the teachings of the Gita to create a balanced financial plan that includes budgeting, saving, and investing ethically. Ensure that your financial goals align with your core values and spiritual principles.

Charitable Giving: Make charitable donations a regular part of your financial plan. Support causes that resonate with your values and contribute to the welfare of society.

Ethical Investments: Choose investments that are socially responsible and align with your ethical beliefs. Avoid investments in companies or industries that engage in harmful or unethical practices.

Simple Living: Practice simplicity and minimalism in your lifestyle. Focus on needs rather than wants, and find contentment in non-material aspects of life.

Regular Reflection: Periodically reflect on your financial decisions and their alignment with your values. Adjust your plan as needed to ensure that you remain true to the principles of the Gita.

Incorporating these teachings into your financial life can lead to greater peace, fulfillment, and a sense of purpose. The Bhagavad Gita offers timeless wisdom that, when applied, can transform the way you view and manage money, making it a tool for positive change rather than a source of stress and conflict

www.ingramcontent.com/pod-product-compliance
Lightning Source LLC
Chambersburg PA
CBHW070357230526
45471CB00006B/2612